Praise for *Ghostlit*

"The poems of Theodora Ziolkowski's *Ghostlit* ripple with such self-assured strength that it is impossible not to feel stronger and more resolute for having read them. Humming with myth and memory, Ziolkowski laces lines with chiffon and sunflower petals, carves and crafts these poems toward an exhilarating freedom. Ziolkowski writes, 'Pompeii was destroyed because of the direction the wind was blowing.' And isn't that the truth. But as often as the wind brings destruction, it carries you from it. Allow these poems to be the wind that carries you to safety and a new softness."

—KAYLEB RAE CANDRILLI

"In *Ghostlit*, Theodora Ziolkowski considers a history of emotional abuse and trauma through the transformative lens of memory. Here, the degradation and pain of a past marriage erupt into the present, just as the knowledge of the present circles the past, always refiguring it, always trying to understand. Ziolkowski is a master of tight narrative, of gothic energy, of intense psychological insight. Reading *Ghostlit* is like inhabiting a brilliant mind—a mind that, for all this, never fails to be interesting, to be complex, and to be powerful."

—KEVIN PRUFER

"Theodora Ziolkowski's poems glow with the ghosts of past selves. From the unhappy wife to the woman abroad questing desire amidst the burning Notre Dame Cathedral, the speaker breaks her desire free from the leash of marriage and yearns for a new life that doesn't begin in lies. Alive with longing and introspection, Ziolkowski's poems bring bright relief to the speaker's mind and make room for a 'woman to rescue herself from the mundanity of the indoors.' From stubborn and messy selves, her ghosts charge into definition by souring the past with fresh eyes. *Ghostlit* is a haunting and astonishing collection that shimmers with love for the salt and flesh of desire."

—SEBASTIÁN H. PÁRAMO

"A spellbinding, liminal, and unflinching collection, Theodora Ziolkowski's *Ghostlit* interweaves themes of memory, myth, identity, trauma, and absence. These superbly crafted poems operate like a triple-fugue offering whose fractured narrator sifts through lost worlds and shifts of consciousness to mend the heroine's splintered soul. Astounding, visceral, and, at heart, poignant."

—HÉLÈNE CARDONA

GHOSTLIT

GHOSTLIT

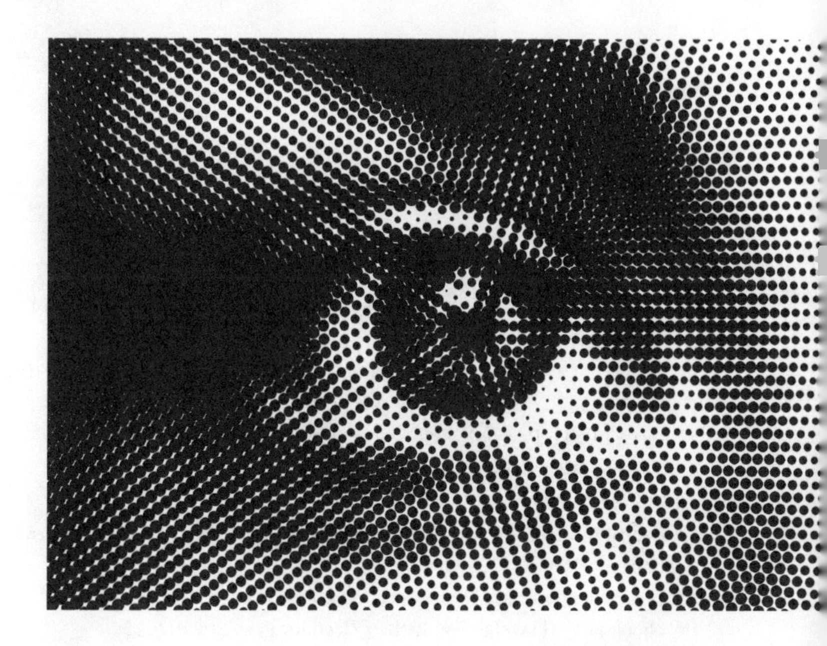

POEMS

THEODORA ZIOLKOWSKI

TRP: THE UNIVERSITY PRESS OF SHSU
HUNTSVILLE, TEXAS 77341

Library of Congress Cataloging-in-Publication Data

Names: Ziolkowski, Theodora, 1989- author.
Title: Ghostlit : poems / Theodora Ziolkowski.
Description: First edition. | Huntsville : TRP: The University Press of SHSU, [2025]
Identifiers: LCCN 2024022251 (print) | LCCN 2024022252 (ebook) | ISBN 9781680034103 (trade paperback) | ISBN 9781680034110 (ebook)
Subjects: LCSH: Psychological abuse victims--Poetry. | Marriage--Psychological aspects--Poetry. | Abused women--Poetry. | LCGFT: Poetry.
Classification: LCC PS3602.I7656 G46 2025 (print) | LCC PS3602.I7656 (ebook) | DDC 811/.6--dc23/eng/20240516
LC record available at https://lccn.loc.gov/2024022251
LC ebook record available at https://lccn.loc.gov/2024022252

FIRST EDITION

Author photo by Lee Upton
Cover design by Cody Gates, Happenstance Type-O-Rama
Interior design by Maureen Forys, Happenstance Type-O-Rama

Printed and bound in the United States of America

First Edition Copyright: 2025

TRP: The University Press of SHSU
Huntsville, Texas 77341
texasreviewpress.org

For
CeCe

CONTENTS

III

IV

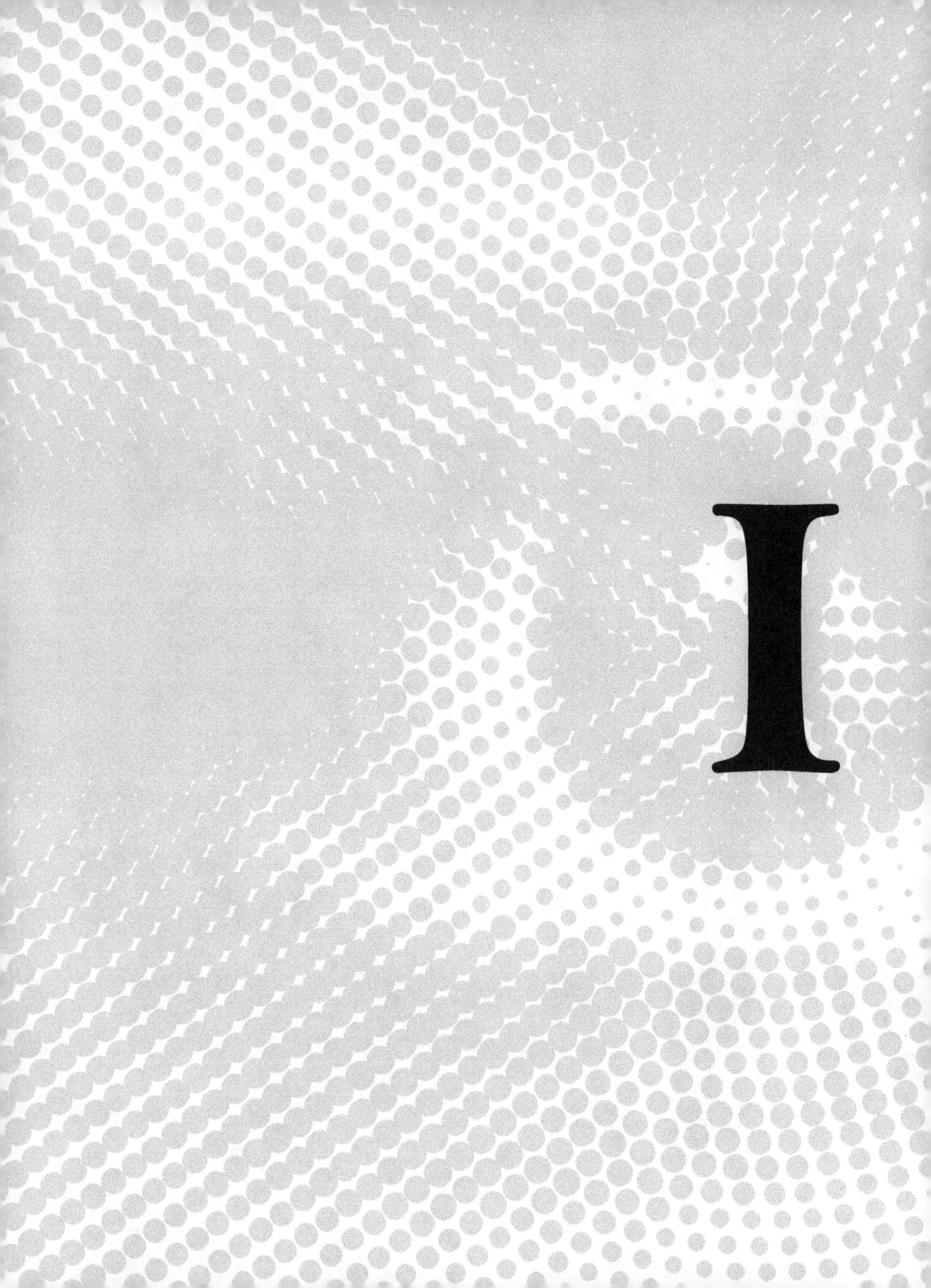
I

Immediately after we wed, I saw a snake

divide the grass. The recessional hymn

was still playing when he picked up that snake
& shook it in my face—

the joke was on me.

Soon, he would strum
the xylophone of my ribcage,

the bones protrusive as keys.

Back then, I was just a body
that needed feeding.

Indulge me.

For some time, I dreamed
I saw my groom in the mirror

he held to my face.

This went on for days, then weeks.
It's natural that a man

who has been wounded

by the image of his girl
shutting the door behind her

is the same man who searches

my eyes & smiles sadly,
suggests that I could have tried harder.

Now the snake at our wedding lives

in my memory.
We hadn't even crossed the threshold.

He was already playing me.

At the memory care center, the residents don't want to make Valentines

Still, I cut hearts with child-safe scissors.
I was a surgeon, Reid sullenly declares as he colors.
He fights to stay in the lines.
Meanwhile, Edith has spilled the glue
& Nell wants to start her card over.
My lap is piled with hearts
so I hum *Blue Moon*
because a familiar tune calms them
the way my bringing home bouquets once did for me.
I'd leave that Target with my cart packed with groceries,
setting sunflowers in the passenger seat beside me.
Now the residents are singing louder,
but I am still cruising along some dark road in Alabama,
breathing in the rotting mouths of those flowers,
when the former surgeon puts his hand on my wrist.
Don't get carried away, he says, taking my scissors.
I lift my foot off the gas.

Before I became the wife, I'd get down on my haunches

to feed the hens in the coop.
They preferred when I was on their level.
Most days, I took my place at the table
with dirt on my face.

Though his father installed a stove
to warm the henhouse through the winter,
their beaks & claws would turn blue,
drop off. In dreams, the stove caught fire

& devoured the coop. I distracted myself
by making my body useful.
He showed me how to drill the trunks
& run the lines. The trees would ooze

as temperatures rise.
In his absence, the sugar house boiled
& the beehive reached full capacity.
Barn swallows lured mates with their song

while the woods echoed with hunters' shots.
I wore an orange cap & vest on my walks.
For weeks, the flutter of wings & feathers,
the hum of insects & of course my choice

of honey or syrup on the pancakes
his mother fixed every Sunday for breakfast.
In the garden, I pulled carrots & peppers,
beans & heirloom tomatoes, but sometimes forgot

about the snakes twisting the bases of plants—
I recoiled before I remembered they're just rubber,
there to fend off the birds & rabbits.
I was only there to pick the food that he ate.

Picture this: you wear girl-sized clothes the summer

your aunt passes down that porcelain doll. You are twenty-four; it is a family heirloom. He carries your gift on the return flight from Michigan. There is no room in his suitcase. Besides, the doll is delicate. The science says you can't think straight if your brain isn't getting enough protein. The doll requires a cabin seat. You do your homework. The chocolate protein shakes are less chalky than vanilla. You have always been a good student though this time it is hard to be. The doll would need to get used to the heat. Every day you think: *So much is wrong with me.* You can see yourself waving as he passes through security, the doll tucked under his arm, but you don't trust that memory. You put the doll on the mantel for everyone to see, but it is mostly just you there & you are so changed. For four years, you & he live in a college town that neither of you can ever quite claim. Even when you are smiling, your face is a broken plate. Morning is the only time of day to run without collapsing from the heat. Before sunup & chocolate shakes, before he wakes, you jog around your complex until you lose feeling.

Having returned from a trip, I found the lake

seemed less blue   & more dramatic   chopped sapphire
I unwrapped a cup from our move   The newspaper I'd used to pack it
told of a dead woman found in a hotel
freezer   (that was the headline)   I know that story
& think of her
often   Later, when the scallops arrive   in dry ice
I wear a baseball glove on one hand   an oven mitt
on the other   to remove the plump discs   furred
with frost   I still need to rinse out the cup
& crumple the paper   The woman supposedly died
from alcohol poisoning   not to mention
hypothermia   which begins but does not end
with shivering   Last week, I was wandering
around Notre Dame Cathedral   & yesterday   it was on fire
Before my trip, I replayed the footage
at the airport   Three beehives near the church roof survived
Now I boil water & watch the teabag bloat
According to their keeper   the bees were responsible
for 165 lbs of honey   Each year
I fold the article about the dead girl   neat as a hankie
& tuck it in my underwear drawer   *It's personal,*
says the Parisian interviewed on TV   She resembles a cat
wrapped in scarves   Another mourns
the cathedral was like a parent   *Losing her was like losing*
a mother, the translator says with earnestness   Did he know
that scallops swim by propelling
themselves?   They open & close their shells   (the only
bivalve mollusk to do this)   You can't leave them
on the heat for too long   They'll turn into rubber   I drown
the scallops in honey   The recipe calls for four garlic cloves
but I have a sweet tooth   & never stopped   associating garlic
with vampires   I tug on a robe & slippers, coil my neck
in scarves as I suck   the soft fishy purses   standing over
the stove   Now the lake has shriveled
in on itself   & my body is an island   forgets how to float

I add Four Roses Bourbon   to the cup   that still smells like our old house
        & everyone wants a piece of the cathedral   *Spira, spera,* wrote Victor Hugo
now that its spire   puckered from the attic   "The forest" under the roof
        it's called   though all the trees cut for its wood   are gone
Sometimes I worry   I will shrug my skin off   like a coat
        as I dream   I fall asleep beside the Häagen-Dazs in a freezer
where the tilapia filets are stacked   like Lincoln Logs
        I think to my dream self: *Stupid,*
where are your clothes?   Sometimes victims of hypothermia are discovered
        nude   It's always cold in some part of the world

For days, the sunflowers watch me

For days, I am charged with an awareness
that they were clipped
from their roots & delivered
to my door in blue plastic
like a body in a body bag.

Their thick stems, the heaviness
of their heads, is obscene—
I drop them in a vase.
How to comprehend
that each head carries an ovary?

Years ago, at the farmer's market,
a vendor who took a shine to my husband
put her hand on my stomach,
looked at him & asked,
How much longer?

What comes first in this telling—
the mind, or the body?
See now how each brown eye
begins to close on the iris.
My hand touches my throat.

Day after day, I watch
the seeds become dust.

The necks fall first.

Eurydice, the seamstress who laced me

into those chutes of organza
shared her name with that gown.

Seasons have come & gone
since I tried Eurydice on & she became
no longer available. That is, on the web,

the designer replaced her
with another cut from a different cloth.
New Eurydice is leaner,

almost see-through in chiffon.
She has a slit up the thigh
to make some bride desired

& I want her. Look now
how my mouth can perform
a decent imitation

of some virgin's smile.
I am not traditional.
I do not keep Eurydice

in our house.
After we exchanged vows,
we fed each other cake

but I ate all the flowers.
In photos from our wedding day,
I look puffed in whipped cream.

What can I say?
Eurydice was steam-pressed into a box

& I can never control myself.

Once, we saw barn swallows fucking, & the pendulum sweep

of that male's beating wings became
a violent choreography.

I remember watching
him & his mom point to the sky,
laughing. I remember

lowering my gaze
& finding it glinting

from my cup of black coffee.
It's only nature—
one, or maybe

both mother & son cooed
as the doves' wings beat harder—
Now how am I to explain

that even before we married,
I was drawn under his wing,
& that the entire time

the male danced around
her, the female faced the trees.

Though I always took Plan B before we had a chance for a baby

My cravings belonged to a pregnant woman.
I told myself I owed my body
the late-night bowls of Cheerios,
the potato chips on Italian bread with butter—
disgusting. Still, nothing satisfied me.
I wandered the house in my bathrobe, jaw working,
& maybe that's what longing is about: a desire to satisfy
what you lack with your mouth.
I smile hardest when I am in control of myself. Most days,
the residents won't retain
my name, but some call me *darling* or *baby.*
They have their own fantasies.
Tonight, after the film about the couple
whose vacation ends badly, I cue up a recording
of snowfall on YouTube.
I won't see the residents or him this week,
& because they rarely recall
my history, the next time I'm with them
will be another opportunity to give them the *Reader's Digest* version
of me. Now the recording crackles
like fistfuls of paper & the montage of snow wipes my screen.
For years, I couldn't put my finger
on our pattern, understand why the light
always seemed flattened.
The article I clip to the inside of my journal reads:
In dementia care, everyone lies.
Later, when I find myself in the kitchen,
every piece of fruit in the bowl is too ripe.

Our apartment still aromatic with the trout lily

I woke the morning after our anniversary
to learn he'd spent the night ill without me.

I couldn't help but blame our wedding cake,
its sugar & buttercream,
which I'd thawed from the freezer
& divided down the middle.

The cake tasted nothing
like it had at our wedding, but he still cleaned
both plates & got food poisoning.

Listen, when I talk about that cake, I am talking about
how in the months that followed, crows replaced
the barn swallows. How one day while jogging
I watched a hawk tear open a rabbit.

Sometimes the old shame rises
& I am reminded of the years I went missing

in a stranger's body.
One night, a storm shook entire branches
from the oak across the street.
When he asked how it was possible

the noise hadn't woken me, I reminded him
what he himself had said: I sleep like the dead.

II

It turns out that the years I believed myself lucky

were partly responsible for my thinking
there was something deeply wrong with me.

I had everything
but was so unhappy,

the ground opening
before I could push

the cart to my car, unload groceries.
Shifting tectonic plates form mountains & oceans.

When an internet quiz asks
my preference, I can't decide

what to answer, next question.
My concern with manholes

has to do with my keys & phone.
What would happen if I happened

to drop either down some manhole?
For so long I thought I did not know

how to do things on my own,
I was incapable. *Really?*

he'd say when I'd tell him
a story & the result

was my leaving the room
cold before he could correct me.

At the memory care center,
the residents call bullshit

on this approach.
They are adults. Do not treat

them like children.
In Houston, I am still waiting

to have a flat tire, but I've already
had my car towed twice.

There are so many potholes
but I know how to raise

my car with the jack.
The year I began dropping

things, I tried to reduce
the space I took up.

This is not a metaphor.
I did starve myself.

My story made a definitive shift
& we each revised our reasons for it.

The narrative of our relationship
was part of the problem.

I got used to being on the bottom,
my every move remarked

upon & examined.
Years after my eating disorder,

I almost sliced open my palm.
I was waiting

to be told I was holding
the knife wrong.

Whenever fruit flies filled
our apartment,

I forgot what I liked & did
not, who I was before I married,

whose unhappiness this was.
A household hack for catching gnats:

Lure them with a mixture
of vinegar, sugar, & soap.

The residents are prone
to walking into each other's rooms.

You have to watch them,
but do not try to control.

Whatever they have taken
can be returned.

Dignity is the state of being
worthy of respect.

I keep consulting the dictionary.
Now my second-guessing controls me.

The visible difference
between a healthy brain

& a brain with dementia
comes down to shrinking tissues.

How often did his control
feel like an extra set of hands

groping the faucet & sponge
while I stood at the kitchen sink

with my own arms submerged?
In the house where I grew up,

I trace the spines of fairy tale books,
gaze into plastic eyes

of stuffed bears that stare
from my childhood bedroom.

Romance is *a feeling of excitement or mystery*
associated with love,

but I see now that I can only relate
to the mystery part.

When I am back
in Houston & haul my things

to my new house,
he will not be there to check

for roaches or peel back webs.
The gnats will petrify in the glass.

The furniture will be at a slant.
When we first moved,

we christened the master closet,
but when I carry the last box

into my new apartment,
in my fist will be the key.

I will hum some song about the moon
I sing with the residents,

the lyrics always a combination
that epitomizes a romance that the singer

could never quite grasp.
Believe me when I say

that when I lie down in bed,
I will touch myself fiercely.

Everything needs to be blessed.

I got used to church bells & sun showers

lunchtime Chardonnay with seafood salad,
the feeling of being so alive it hurt.
In Rome, that old self who ate like a bird
& professed to feel full was gone—
Even catcalls proved I wasn't a ghost,
I wanted to be seen. A year after I got better, I hungered
to belong to something, & occasionally prayed
outside the Vatican, where hawkers pressed bottled water
at my elbow & every Wednesday the Pope appeared
on the balcony to bless the city. Attendants guarding St. Peter's
offered women paper shawls to drape bare shoulders,
but I dipped my fingers into the baptismal font,
pretending not to see the hand shaking that shawl
as I made the sign of the cross.
I don't know what I was wearing.
I know I was not properly covered up.

Leaving Vatican City, I was packed shoulder to shoulder

& jostled against rain-slicked arms & knapsacks
when I felt a hand groping my ass, then another
reaching up my dress.

For a moment, I thought it was an accident.
Then I turned & saw the glance
the men exchanged. They were a team.
Who would see what they were doing?

You are safe in your body, a friend had said
when I told her I felt as if somewhere
someone was walking around

in my body. Who was she?
A doctor warned I was in danger
of not being able to have children,
then provided a list of experts.

You'd think dining would be easy
but heaped plates glared, unappetizing.
Meanwhile, I impressed my ballet teacher

by what a perfect line
I could *chaîné* across the floor.
The trick is knowing how to spot.
You turn your head with your body,

train your gaze to prevent dizziness.
I chose a point in the mirror
to traverse the studio

as my teacher told the littlest dancers
what they saw required practice.
It took years to get healthy.
I pulled the cord to signal my stop.

Pushing my way out of the crush,
I turned to find what remained
of the men's faces had blurred into nothing.

Just as I stepped off,
another woman stepped on.

When we were making our descent, some rock rolled into my path

At the bottom of Mount Vesuvius, the trees were black.
The grove of seared branches made me think I was still in bed

with my face in my hands. When he joined me that week,
Italy seemed louder, the moon cast shadows.
Sharing *insalata di polpo* on that terrace in Sorrento,

I forgot how to swallow.
Meanwhile, boys in Amalfi drew nets of redfish.

Men hacked trees while I peeled oranges,
watched my fingertips bleed. What if I had fallen
on that rock like he thought
I would. Or was it that he proposed it & didn't

worry, or that he assumed my losing my footing
was inevitable—the decline was something I couldn't handle?
So often I thought I was at risk for something

I could not control. Mount Vesuvius, for example.
Tourists can photograph the smoke & ashes.
Understand that the journey up is different
from down. Are there rules for addressing a body

that's neither on nor under ground? That eruption
buried Pompeii. On my phone, I carry photos

of the remains: plaster poured into pockets of ash
to recreate the victims' shapes.
For years, I tried to hold together a body

that had already come apart. Pompeii was destroyed
because of the direction the wind was blowing.

The wife could not open her mouth to justify herself

Her husband hid his hatred so completely,
it was hard for her to see herself clearly.

To justify herself,
she ruminated on a pair of scissors.

It was hard for her to see herself clearly.
Every night was vodka tonics & razors

when she'd ruminate on a pair of scissors
& her husband so completely hid his hatred.

Every night was vodka tonics & razors.
To justify herself, the wife would not open her mouth.

It was on a balcony over the Mediterranean that I found myself slurping the bodies

The properties of aerodynamics
demand you tilt an oyster shell
with the wide end
to your lips, then chew

once, twice at the most
to preserve the flavor
So salty in the back
of my throat

I did not know the etiquette
For a long time, I was used
to being swallowed

An oyster that refuses to open
is most likely dead
I was on a beach
an hour outside Rome
tang of beer & Aperol
alive on my tongue

Nero's Castle was on the opposite
end of the shore

He murdered his wife
while the city burned
For years, my body was filled with mirrors

My tongue wore down my incisors
Bats could be birds & vice versa

That day, I passed
every hour on the shore

Charging into the sea, my breath caught
before I went under
In my favorite stories,
a woman rescues herself
from the mundanity of being indoors

A rock slit my leg
when the sea was choppy

When the lifeguard cleaned off the blood
I shivered

The ball of my foot
in his hands & my hand
on his shoulder

I was drunk & lightheaded
to have my brokenness visible

For so long I did not want to be touched

My husband placed the hook

To be a wife was to be taught

I was a tall order

I was so afraid no one would believe me
when I explained why I wanted
to leave what I was afraid
I needed

My mouth was only good
for so much

He could not be
with the old version of me

I saw the red bloom in the water
& hoisted myself onto the jetty

Now I am this woman, I thought

Unclear what woman I meant by "this"

How tender to be mended,
In Rome, birds/bats flanked the clotheslines
outside my window

Desire was a leash

Across the ocean, I could be myself

He told me I needed his counsel

Oysters are hermaphroditic
but 90% end up female

Their sex is never inevitable

Before bed & even after I woke,
he'd say I was *all talk*

According to him, I was much better
now that I was more
like him

Does she or I deserve to be buried?

On the beach,
it was like a switch went off
I considered leaving
but thought I knew nothing

He loved me

Why call me stiff?

My strand of black pearls
I wear around both wrists

After the lifeguard applied the bandage
I returned to the water

I floated

In the months that followed,
I cultivated small rituals
that brought me back
to that summer,

drank doll-sized cups
of espresso & drizzled olive oil
on morning toast instead of butter

Most pearls are harvested
from inedible oysters

The way I understood marriage
came down to how

I made my bed
& now must lie in it

I told no one
that while life roared with him,
something broke inside me

My last oyster, I recognized
myself in the slime

As the ocean is governed by wind,
oysters are shaped by their beds

Our marriage reflected that

He wanted us to have sons in particular

Forget that my uterus
is filled with bats

I know I will be punished for this

In the dream in which I refuse to repair us

Some boy band blares from a boombox
& paper lanterns sway from trees.
This party is not as fun as I expected.
Someone says something terrible;
the piñata spills tootsie pops exclusively.
I am wearing a corset
so all the men will love me.
I must do better at smiling.
I cannot be interesting forever.
Here, my husband & I are both manipulators,
& he wants to know the answer
to the question I ask myself
every day: *What made you this way?*
Though the party is almost over,
he is still pouring champagne
into the same plastic cup
where I left my fingernail clippings.
Excuse me, I say.
Then make myself small
in another man's arms.

The best part of a descent is looking up

The wife cannot hear herself
over the continual plucking of his harp.

It's a lyre, he'd remind her.
Liar, she'd repeat,

like a doll with a pull-string.
O vulnerability,

she feels bad for herself.
Her husband was angry

she was not aroused.
I could have had some other life,

she tells three dog heads,
yet while she examines her rotting

arms, her legs, she flatters herself
that she is dead.

Down here, even dead
bodies contain heat,

& these bad dogs won't stop barking.

Lying in the hospital bed, I wonder why every song I love

contains the word *bitch*.
Then the nurse takes my hand,
asks if I want to watch TV.

I am my most vulnerable
waiting for surgery.

Thatta girl, she socks my feet.
Her tone is congratulatory,
my smock a snowbank

gaping at the back,
red ties bowed into winterberries—

there is poison inside me.
Normally, I crank the volume
up on my headphones,

but today that's unnecessary
as I will be sleeping.

I can't stop thinking
about those songs I play
as the doctor peers inside me.

According to Google,
bitches were originally trained

to sniff out prey.
Then they were expected
to keep the house clean,

lest a mole expose
them as bitches & thus destine

those witches to burn at the stake.
I have never felt
more inside of my body

as when I found myself
without my husband, alone

in another country.
Now the nurse searches
my arm for a vein, & I consider

how there is no gray area:
The bitch in every song I love

is either adored or hated.
Cue audience applause
as the nurse changes the channel

& a woman ices a cake on TV.
Bitches mean dogs,

but *to bitch* means complaining.
i.e. The wife bitches about endless
piles of laundry. *Unfortunately, there is no way*

to remove your nose ring, the doctor proclaims.
i.e. There is an occasion

though not likely
for radiation burning.
Please sign & initial your understanding.

It ought to have been a sign
that marriage turned

my initials into the shorthand
for a disease evinced by blood
coughed into handkerchiefs,

& that ending my time as his wife
made me prone to reclaiming

the years I was silenced.
This is where we'll be extracting,
the doctor holds a diagram

to explain, but practice
makes me translate her science

into the same anxiety
I carried that first night
I felt a hand at my waist,

then registered the absence of a ring.
I poured myself a glass of white wine

& laughed my ass off
at that party. Kept my bitching
behind my teeth—

Time to be wheeled away,
& the nurse squeezes my hand

with a tenderness
that makes my throat ache.
I once saw a performance

where the singer wanders
through a bright forest
of ethereal birches

until disease devours the plot
as her bitch dogs bark.

I often wonder for how long
those bad cells were a part
of me. I mean, at what point

did they take a turn for the worse?

III

I was five & running errands with my mother

Kmart was the one-stop-shop for you-name-it,
& at that age I refused to wear anything but a dress

as on Easter I donned one shell-pink, skirt tiered.
I wore a straw bonnet with it, my Mary Jane shoes. Later,
someone who saw a picture of me in that outfit said to my mother

it's too big, it doesn't fit her. At Kmart, I played lost in the labyrinth
of aisles, my behavior rewarded with Kmart Café:
patty robed in American cheese, lettuce like a slimed doily I loved.

When I married, the bouquet I carried, then tossed,
was in memory of my grandmother, Rose. Laying her down,

roses cast the ground —
        beauty that clothes a stone.

That morning, he kept his distance: blackout curtains, no breakfast

Wind howled through the long
dark throat of the fraternity.

Go on, get up, said the boy.

In the bathroom, my breath made frost.
Some girl's lipstick streaked the tile
& beer bottles lined the sink.

Artwork of my cocktail dress on the floor:
clot of black poppies

at the bottom of a pond.

Push the body to recover
a recognizable rhythm
& its breath evens:

mascara to lashes, my hand shaking—
Sometimes memories worth forgetting

turn into stories that want

different endings.
Like the part when I zipped up
my boots & the frat door

shut like a jaw. Or like how after
I climbed the frozen hill to campus

to dance before a class

that studied the way I moved
my bruised body,
the mirror laughed

back my choreography.
Can a mind that fails to recall

also belong to a body

that remembers everything?
Years after, & it doesn't matter
if I wake beside

a man who loves me.
When I least expect it,

I rise as that same

girl on a sour mattress,
her body responding to a ghost

of that boy's hard gaze.

Every summer, you read *Middlemarch* but never make it past the middle

What loneliness is more lonely than distrust?

—GEORGE ELIOT, *MIDDLEMARCH*

What season is lonelier than summer? Come August, the palm trees undress beneath your window; bark sloughs & gasoline kaleidoscopes the footpath you run. You are good about replenishing the canned goods; you are prepped for hurricanes & floods. Loneliness clips a leash around your throat. Remember the graffiti on I-45 that would shout BE SOMEONE on your commute to school, then how lonely it was to be someone you can't trust? Now recall how you once kept a mirror in your glovebox, a reaction to that time you offered a man your mind & he studied it for a very long time, then walked away—

Recently, there has been an infestation of crows

Today they fill the sky like cutouts
of black paper When my sister visits
neither she nor I can hear the other over the barking
dogs in the park We keep talking We walk
the path behind my apartment until we can no longer feel
our legs I prefer public
transportation if the distance is too great but am private
in most other ways The wolf wants to eat
the girl & the girl's
grandma His coat can't be
removed with the ease of the girl's hood
It took months of living in Houston before I was willing to climb
behind a wheel I like to be in motion the sun rising
the part of morning that is still
dark my car the only car on the road
lone wolf There is no stopping
Every light burns green When I think of the riding
part of Little Red's hood I think
of the wolf Little Red
Wolf Hood I used to get trashed
but like a good girl left
my car I had in mind
which man would put a roof
over my head until I was sober enough
to take the wheel
again Once while shopping
my cart was stopped
with a hand I looked like the man's first
love, he was sorry for staring
I have her eyes *Is she dead?*
I wanted to ask There are no woods
in our suburb in Houston though some boast
"nature paths" I wake
to groans of school buses *Good girl,*
our neighbor's second-grade son kneels

to pat his dog The lab only recognizes
G-bye She does not know when to stop
when no means no
how to sit girl, sit The bitch
does not understand what the boy means when he pushes her
down on her haunches *Bad*
I have more selfies of my sister & me than I have photos
of anything Today we snap funny faces the crows swarm the backdrop
the sky breaks open & we pull up our hoods
The first time I saw a dead crow was on my honeymoon
I found it on the doorstep of our cabin We had been horseback riding
in the mountains Really
I was given a pony *Tiny horse for a tiny*
person, the tour guide said as I swung
my leg around the saddle After I saw that crow
I glanced up to find a startled woman staring back
It had flown into the glass door that my husband slid back
Don't kill it, I blurted a reflex
In the jacuzzi I drew my tired legs to my chest
The lip of the tub was guarded by towels
wrangled into swans The water smelled like hay & apples
My pony had been no match for the cliffs It could not keep up
with my husband's stallion I am not a small person
Sometimes before bed while I rifle through the day's events
I consider the choices I had & how often I chose
wrongly When the Uber arrives, my sister runs ahead
I find red strands in my brush a pillowcase stained
from her hair dye My sister sends me her driver's information,
I time her journey & keep every screenshot of his license plate
Every morning, I run hoodie drawstrings
knotting my chin I count each breath
I never tame my desire I feed it
like a pet Long ago, I scratched away every mirror
pressed my paws together tongued
a tiny claw lodged between my teeth I was never good at seeing myself
clearly I never know
how to stop telling myself the same story

At the memory care center, the parlor resembles

what was once my grandmother's bedroom
but with artificial flowers.
Dixie cups swirl with pink ice cream,
the coffee table is flecked with powdered creamer,
O my teeth sing. On the subject of the residents, they all
smell sweet. Chocolate malts & Milk Duds smear their bathrobes
I love you, I say. I adore the order of their
days, the three square meals plus snacks
in between. They forget when they have eaten,
they are always hungry, *No one feeds us,*
complains Jane. We sing the National Anthem whenever we rise
for dinner, follow the leader. *Do you live upstairs?*
They ask every day. The corridors all end the same way.
The mind can resuscitate
anything when it is given enough
room to breathe. When the parking lot glows red, I know
I am in danger of learning
that the bed of a resident may
be empty. None of them asks
to hold hands, but I often find a palm where I swear
my own heart ought to be. The memory
care center faces a street. Not a shift goes by without
Jane pressing her face to the glass & asking
would I like to get out of here,
Shhh she has her car keys.
There is no second story
at the memory care center, there are no
stairs, no elevator. I often trace the walls as I walk.
After I made my mind up about us,
the decision turned inside out.
Still, it is easy to get lost
when every direction ends
at the start. After work, I used to collapse
on the couch. Merlot, Ritz crackers,
crumbs between the cushions

surely. Our place in Houston was all hardwood & slate.
Alone, I'd vacuum compulsively. I hated the marks
of our living in that small space. Gloss of coconut
oil on the counter, his gym sock in the dryer &
somewhere, in the garage, tree ornaments
that never made it back to the box.
Glitter on my fingertips when I wrapped
them in towels. Hershey kiss stale in the mouth
of the knit frog I'd string with mistletoe,
the ultimate "haha," *I love you*
sewn on the curl of frog-
prince tongue. Winter in Houston is always
far off. We moved here for him
but it was never enough. Of the minds of residents,
the handbook suggests
the present can only break
down. Show photos & other mementos
& smile, they can't see what's underneath.
In that suburb in Houston, our bedroom faced a lake.
For a brain with dementia,
gray matter blooms in the area
that isn't already gray.

It's late, your cat is clawing the backseat, & you're afraid your husband will nod off

so sleepy behind the wheel. Southbound, the air still smells of tar & fried okra. The only radio stations are country & gospel—it's as if you've never left. The motel you stop at is run by a man shaped like a bathtub. He greets you in a lobby aglow with gumball machines, a TV. The Waffle House looming over I-59 bathes every view like a yellow moon; your room faces the pool. Inside, you find the bed covered in surprisingly white linen. He scours for bed bugs while you shower, recalling the time you & he stayed in an inn filled with mirrors. The night had a triple-digit price tag & the air felt like an argument. Who had been fighting? That trip, you had a friend's wedding to attend & your dress was a tent. At the reception, you pawed the vat of dessert mousse, dress straps sloughing, bodice like a sack while the happy couple danced. *You are a wife*, you told yourself then as you watched the groom spin his bride. *You are the wife*, you think now as you emerge from the shower to join him in bed, in that fleabag motel off the highway you pay cash to sleep in—over & again, you remind yourself that you are the wife, & the refrain will gather momentum, until *you are the wife* is all that you hear when, come morning, your cat noses its way to the pool, where it finds the deer carcass before you do.

From NPR, the wife learns of the hog problem in Texas

the privacy issue with Snapchat
    & the drop in the stock market,

a mass grave discovered
    in Ireland—all babies.

After breaking information
    concerning the latest lost girl,

the wife dials down the radio.

*

Inflatable mattresses are spotted
    flying across Houston.
They tumble into trees & lakes.

*

The wife will be married for five years this summer.
    Suggested presents include wooden clocks
& wooden statues, croquet sets & cedar liners for closets.

A friend suggests the wife could also plan
    a romantic walk in the forest or plant a tree.
Oak symbolizes solidarity.

*

When she orders the black truffle pasta,
        the wife thinks of the hogs.
Her booth faces a sea of couples.
        She'd heard that truffle hogs are trained
with leashes, that the males' sex hormones smell similar
        to the fungus they dig for.

*

Late-night programs are all trying
        to sell her something,

but the wife has no interest
        in the slimming chair or slap chopper.

She is already slim.
        She has no problem fixing salad.

*

According to the report, those Irish babies
        were dumped in graves
after being separated
        from their mothers
who stayed at that convent
        because they didn't have husbands.

*

The wife misses her mother.

*

When a wife is not a mother
        does that make her a wife
more than a daughter?

*

Sometimes the wife wakes as if
        she'd fallen asleep in a tree
or at the bottom of a lake.
        It depends on the day.

*

Her first day on the other side of the country,
        an old love texts the wife a selfie.

The wife has forgotten how to function
        without instructions.
She answers with a photo of her favorite black dress
        spread across her mattress.

*

Ghosts in the wife's world
        equal dead girls.

Her vision is an issue.
Every woman looks dead to her.

*

Her grandmother had glaucoma
so the ophthalmologist gives the wife
the option of a closer examination.
Better to check for traces.
Women carry things.

*

In addition to her name,
the wife changes
her passwords.
She alphabetizes her bookshelves.
She gets a French manicure.

*

For every thought the wife thinks,
a dead girl climbs out of a tree.

*

When she dreams of the forest
it is violent with spring.

Mothers call their daughters.

On the phone, Mom says the deer population continues

to increase up north. Last winter I found one
washed on the shore. The body was missing its legs.
It was all torso & head. When I saw the worn nubs
above its lids, I thumbed my forehead.
I haven't seen one deer in Texas.
Somewhere along SH 30, he photographs me gazing
at sunflowers. My hairdresser tells me she loses interest
in a man after he reciprocates her interest.
I coo as she massages conditioner
into my scalp & the salon becomes a forest.
You know the part in the film when the hero climbs
into the body of a horse? The scene doesn't show
the blow & the sawing, we only see the man
tucked into the belly. The horse's nap isn't even bloody.
Last summer in Italy, I threw myself
from painting to painting,
then studied Caravaggio's *Narcissus*
gazing into the reflection of the stream.
In the mirror, I watch the hairdresser
reach for comb & scissors.
Sometimes I think our desire
comes from something else
entirely, like when a girl accepts the Virgin's key
so of course, her life ends badly.
When he joined me in Italy,
we took a train to the south of the country.
One night I dreamt of old boyfriends
& woke believing they'd dug
out their eyes & left
them beside me.
In Amalfi, the cabbie drove us
round those winding roads,
& at some point we must have taken a selfie
because in that one of us in the backseat,
my eyes are squinting from the flash
while his are looking through me.

In the horror story of my invention, it is the wife's unfocused gaze

that convinces the husband
that his wife isn't
listening. How is he to instruct
her properly

The husband is stroking his beard
& the wife is touching her face

He has the authority
to ask her anything

Close your eyes for me,
please

To whom does she owe
the pleasure
of being dragged
here?

Surely, she won't be the last
he will need to teach

To be in the presence
of his scrutiny
is like dry heaving roses

The husband can't help himself:
Her trumpet swan neck
is a feature on which to feast
as he remembers what's under
her dumb fuzzy cardigan

Heads before stems

Historically speaking,
his word is greater than hers

She says, *I'm sorry, the ghost*
you are calling cannot be reached

So the husband places his hand
on her knee

& when she opens her eyes,
she can see herself wandering
mountains & negotiating
their dangers—
all those opportunities
to drop from a blow
to the head so strong
out bashes your brain—
on every climb
signs warn of falling
rocks but she never
once looked up
Why bother? Rocks
were already falling

IV

At least I feel something, I think, as I run the same route I took

when my head was heavy with vodka tonics
& by God, that night I still ran
beneath dark branches.
My old neighborhood feels different
today, the shut-up carwash florescent,
aqua flourishes on chipped stucco—
I shout at the leaves:
When will I learn my own needs?
Call it whatever, this faith
that today when I spring
alone into the street,
at some point traffic
will have to stop me.

“Do Not Touch Without Assistance” reads the sign at the antique store

so you refrain from touching the glass swan & shove your hands in your pockets. You can still hear that bird shatter. From his perspective, you were always at fault for the children you never tried for. Did you know that swans are the largest migrating birds? Now you are rewriting a novel with the word “swan” in the title. The protagonist is continually falling for men who do everything but treasure her. When an animal is fragile, does that mean it only exists as a spectacle? Leda did not know that swan was really a god fucking with her. Here, in this shop, every antique is wooled with dust. It’s never too late not to touch; no price exists for what you want but it’s why you wake covered in feathers. Swans have an excellent sense of memory, so in this telling, the roles are fluid. You are the swan & he is the woman. To him, you say: *There was a time your hand fit precisely in mine.* Swans remember who has & has not been kind.

In *Sleeping with the Enemy*, Julia Roberts plays a woman whose new life

begins with a lie
The woman's name is Laura
See, the woman she was is dead,
& in death, Laura gets to start again

He called me a liar,
for there I was, a writer

The story can be summarized
by the film's title

Though I'd already wiped down the mirror
he tore off more towels

I always left streaks

Before Laura leaves her husband,
there is the pressure to go sailing
The husband wants her to join him,

but Laura hates sailing
She never learned to swim
(she lets us think)

Years ago, there was a storm
when we took the boat on the lake

My face turned green
I willed myself to sleep

In the dream, I thrashed
to the surface, every inch
of my body, I unbodied

Waking in his arms,
I bobbed to calm waters

Laura jumps ship & swims to a buoy
(She had been learning in secret)

Secrecy is not part of marriage
but it is necessary for escaping

In the opening scene,
the target digs the sand

(*Target* is the term that the literature
calls the person on the receiving end)

In this instance, Laura is the target
She fills a pail with clams

Touch & taste are a clam's only senses

Reborn Laura falls for a man who throws
her around when they dance
He is supposed to be the hero

This is a digression

It's hard to follow
when the roles keep reversing

The Knight in Shining Armor
&, indeed, the husband almost kills her

I got accustomed to believing
I was silently shouting

Instead, I'd lock the door & take the car
I would not look behind me

Understand that a life can be taken
before it is ended

I watched & re-watched the scene
when he finds Laura's wedding ring
then wears it on his pinky,
for they are one

Parting, however, is an option

Reborn Laura's mouth is an *o*
when her husband pulls the trigger

Now I can't stop wiping down my mirror

His wife is not the same

It's Hollywood, so of course
the muzzle wasn't loaded

I chose my own life to save

There is a fact of memory & there is a fact of feeling

There is also a fact of feeling
in my memory
I did
not exist.

Cross this out
& this.

In his videos, look with what precision
my face is agreeable.
The pitch of my voice is higher, I sound childish.
Now everything seems like an omen.

The bat down the chimney
& into the glow of my parents' living room.

    Like a scattered Queen of Night tulip,
    it blew across our heads.

Then there was the four-car pileup
behind me, Mom, & Dad.

    When that Nissan hydroplaned,
    the cargo truck struck our back bumper.
    My head snapped back & forward.

    Watching that Nissan torpedo,
    I thought it squealed like an animal.

Later, Dad remarked on my scream.
That part for me is amnesia.
    Had I seen the bloody face of that teen?

Back in Houston, my neck strained.
Nothing belongs to me, I told myself
as I assembled my new bed.

For hours, I listened to B.B. King croon
about the thrill being gone.

Heaving the mattress atop the frame,
I sang, *I belong to no one.*

I love watching Irish step dancers, their feet tapping

as if jerked by invisible strings. I am good at copying, especially if there is a mirror
in front of me. A cat also learns by imitating. She curls up in her owner's arms.

She sleeps the day away. In the cartoon, Tom's attempts to catch Jerry always end
in disaster. This is funny because in fables we are prepared for the cat to be clever.

Today a woman called our splitting a "death," explaining that when two people
join lives then sever their union, death is the result of its dissolution.

Obviously, a body goes until it doesn't. My husband is the reason
I hole out my wardrobe, give my sister all my old dresses,

then see his hands on the straps & pockets as she models the red one
& asks: *Do you like it?* It's not easy to be left in the dark,

to confront a shade of myself: how I used to set the table with real silver.
How long will it take for my body to become familiar? A cat is a witch's familiar.

The two are meant to stay together. Yes, I did in fact take the cat
& my husband was the one to nail that broomstick above my writing desk.

I now know why I felt trapped. How naturally he appeared every night
in the doorway, light fizzing inside the lamp that he carried.

When I realize what to call it, I ask my therapist

Will each hurt add up?
Will they all become
a nesting box, the largest

holding the others—
will that one be soundproof?

(I only respond to his letters
in my imagination.)

My therapist wants
to make sure I'm not
overwhelmed by metaphors,

but I need a shape
to see things as they are.

(Sometimes the mother rabbit
eats the weakest in the litter.)

I write on my palm:
When was the last time you hurt someone?
For so long I nurtured his hurt

& called it love.
Last week, to defend all my metaphors,

I told a roomful of students I am a visual learner.
(I am used to being the one who has to learn.)

In an article that traces
the cycle of abuse,
the werewolf is considered

the container for the abuser.
His transformation is a cycle.

He deviates with the moon.
A foot out our door

& he said we had to put a face on.
My head hurt.
How often did my response belong to a parrot?

The queen was disappointed
by her reflection's unfairness.

(He wanted me to be a different person.)
Smiling is painful after poison.

To see a princess do housework
is to watch her rearrange the mess.
(On road trips, when I had to use the bathroom

he pushed on my stomach.)
Him at the wheel & me at the window,

discomfort is good,
& in any case, his pushing was a "joke."

I call this a hole.
Now when I arrange flowers,
my hands translate his aesthetic.

(Lately I don't want to change out of pajamas.)
Will closure be what he asks for?

Even the dead don't provide closure.
The ghosts keep coming.

In Montana, a hawk flew over our car,
a rabbit dangling upside down
from its talons

(the stomach of that rabbit curled
like a question mark).

Years after, he dismissed my memory
when I brought up that hawk

& rabbit, but then
when we were watching
the honeymoon footage,

the frame zeroes in on my face
(as I describe to the camera

the same incident the same way).
A hawk flew over our car,

a rabbit dangling…
I use soap & water
to remove my wedding ring.

If taught appropriately,
parrots understand what they're saying.

(On my palm, bright ink of "hurt,"
letters glow like ghosts)—

Let me be clear.
All those times I remained
in parking lots, engine off,

crying silently,
I was nearly erased.

While online dating, Eurydice adds "black trumpet mushrooms"

to her list of "Things that Interest Me."
But the gods want to know, is she the kind of woman

who orders the watercress salad or the 12-ounce prime rib?
It is important to be aware of these distinctions.

As a girl, Eurydice loved to watch films
about the future, especially those that featured zombies

& Apocalypse. How delightful it would be to zip
into a foil suit, live off pockets of flash-frozen food.

There is something calming about the end of the world
as Eurydice's phone buzzes & she likes

another sound clip: *Xoxo, Orpheus.*
Where once Eurydice could see the river,

reeds block the window, damp with loam.
Perhaps she has just been underground too long,

dancing barefoot on broken cutlery.
Maybe, for some god, she could arrange

black trumpet mushrooms on blue dinner plates.

At the memory care center, the waters are calm before they are choppy

& no matter how many times I show them,
they don't understand
how to take
the napkin   where to place

the spoon   *This isn't anything,*
says Karen, *It doesn't*
go anywhere, this
is stupid

At dinner, I cut their chicken into pieces
& feed them

slowly   I don't want Ned to choke,
but he's hungry   Peas roll off his plate

My hand he mistakes
for potato   He draws it to his face

Our survival is based on the existence of holes

He can't find his mouth
It's easier to feed him
than myself   What I love

about the care center are the doilies
& rose wallpaper, dancing with the residents to Elvis Presley

It's a desire for the past I had no part in,
for the King of Rock n' Roll crooning

Most nights, it is like the residents & I are on a ship
with no destination. From the outside,
the lit windows must look like portholes,

while we dine in a Flying Dutchman,
the dinner party just starting

During the tropical storm, my hands scrabbled

tried to make sense   of the sludge
Night after night   wind gnashed the windows
the balcony rails   the carpet
Where did the crows go   The cranes, I imagine
tore the crape myrtle   nested in pink-turned-purple   beaten
down by the deluge   plumage dyed   in metals & oil
my apartment a marsh   of cat fur & teacups rimmed
with my lipstick   why did I wear Cherries in the Snow
if not to impress the walls   Meanwhile
boxed wine on the counter   grew flowers
the flood got   under my skin   In dreams
I waded through Kleenex   The day was the same as night
because darkness   but what does time matter
when you are alone   facing windows
like portholes   looking onto a sky
made of tar   leaves splattering from treetops   ink staining
the sidewalk   as if all this time   we were wrong
the trees are not made   of water & bark   Every day while helicopters
blared, I brushed my hair with leaves   trees shed onto the balcony
Here is the church   & here is the steeple   whatever you do
don't open the doors   Dear radio   what is a storm
but a sickness   So you see I was high
in my tower   the swimming pool below   like clouded dishwater
& when I saw the boys   smoking on the balcony
I welcomed the pot   its underground scent   I first tried it
in a hot tub with friends   & said it was like thinking
through alphabet soup   before the boy
who passed the blunt   curled his guitar-calloused fingers
round my waist & asked   What's the matter
princess   aren't you high enough for this yet?
Come landfall   I wanted to drop to my knees
become more than the girl   with the wick & the flame
but a selkie   each a woman   who masters her skin
makes love to the dark   & swims

Lying on the patient table—gel on the wand

& the wand inside me—
I am looking at the screen
& the doctor is looking
for poison. Listen closely.
Some women go to hell
& come back without
turning the other cheek.
Every dream asks
for a reckoning.
View from inside me:
Nothing registers my touch
yet everything can touch me
is a memory.
Now Houston is on the lip
of a long green spring.
A bundle of bad cells
has the capacity
to grow & attack the body.
With a turn of a wand,
the ultrasound refutes
ghosts entirely.
He is not part of my world
& I am no longer in sight
of his perceptions—
I pull on my street clothes.
The door leads skyward.

Acknowledgments

I am grateful to the editors of the following publications, in which versions of these poems, often under different titles, first appeared:

Apple Valley Review: "I love watching Irish step dancers, their feet tapping"

Arts & Letters: "I was five & running errands with my mother" ('Ensemble')

Bayou Magazine: "In the dream in which I refuse to repair us"

Bending Genres: "Every summer, you read *Middlemarch* but never make it past the middle"

COMP, an interdisciplinary journal: "Picture this: you wear girl-sized clothes the summer," "Leaving Vatican City, I was packed shoulder to shoulder," "It's late, your cat is clawing the backseat, & you're afraid your husband will nod off," "There is a fact of memory & there is a fact of feeling," and "At the memory care center, the waters are calm before they are choppy"

december magazine: "Eurydice, the seamstress who laced me" and "Immediately after we wed"

Josephine Quarterly: "Having returned from a trip, I found the lake"

Lake Effect: "The best part of the descent is looking up"

New Orleans Review: "More than her doped mouth, it is her unfocused gaze" ('History')

New South Journal: "It was on a balcony over the Mediterranean that I found myself"

Oxford Poetry: "When we were making our descent, some rock rolled into my path"

Plant-Human Quarterly: "For days, the sunflowers watch me"

Power of the Feminine "I": An Anthology: "Though I always took Plan B before we had a chance for a baby"

Prairie Schooner: "Recently, there has been an infestation of crows" ('Riding')

Radar Poetry: "Lying on the patient table—gel on the wand" (reprinted in *Medmic: Conversations, Culture & Creativity from the Healthcare Community)*

Rattle: "At the memory care center, the residents don't want to make Valentines"

2River View: "On the phone, Mom says the deer population" and "Our apartment still aromatic with the trout lily"

Rogue Agent: "The morning, the boy kept his distance: blackout curtains, no breakfast"

Slipstream: "The wife could not open her mouth to justify herself"

Sweet Lit: "At the memory care center, the parlor resembles"

West Review: "At least I feel something, I think, as I run the same route I took"

Thank you, always, to my family and friends: You make me a better writer and a much better person.

I am profoundly grateful to TRP for choosing *Ghostlit.* Thank you, J, PJ, and Charlie.

Immense gratitude to the University of Houston Creative Writing Program. To my teachers at UH, especially: Kevin Prufer, Antonya Nelson, Alex Parsons, Sally Connolly, Robert Boswell, Peter Turchi, Michael Snediker, and J. Kastely. To my dazzlingly brilliant peers, who read earlier iterations of these poems and this manuscript with care: Niki Herd, Liza Watkins, Devereux Fortuna, Gabriella Iacono, Erik Brown, Aris Kian, Brittny Ray Crowell, and Kaitlin Rizzo.

My gratitude to Inprint, whose generosity helped provide necessary writing time.

Matt Bell: Thank you for reading an earlier draft of this manuscript and for your support over the years.

Thank you to Chelsea B. DesAutels for the (always) revelatory generative poem exchanges, and for reading many versions of the poems that appear in these pages. I am forever grateful for your friendship.

Warm thanks to the English Department and to my colleagues at the University of Nebraska at Kearney.

Everything I write is in memory of my grandmother, Rose; my grandfather, Charlie; my aunt, Lana; my uncle, Joe; my cousin, Carla; and, most recently, my cousin, Brittany; my beloved grandparents, Yetta and Theodore Ziolkowski; and my aunt, Alice Faye Upton, who I miss every day.

Thank you, Ralph and Candace Burns, for your love and steadfast support.

Thank you, always, to my parents. I am wildly fortunate to be your daughter. I will never be able to thank you enough.

Will, you are everything and more and then some. Thank you for being on this adventure with me. I love you.

This book has been dedicated to my sister, CeCe—my forever best friend—from the day its first poem was penned.